Comptroller of the Currency
Administrator of National Banks

National Banks *and*

The Dual Banking System

SEPTEMBER 2003

National Banks and
The Dual Banking System

SEPTEMBER 2003

Today, the dual banking system, which has been a hallmark of banking in the United States for nearly 200 years, is under attack, as many states have attempted to assert legislative and enforcement authority over national banks in a way that contradicts constitutional principles that have been well-settled since the early nineteenth century.

This paper explains the history and features of the "dual banking system" and discusses the judicial and legislative precedents establishing the constitutional limits on the ability of states to control or direct national bank powers conferred under federal law.

The "dual banking system" refers to the parallel state and federal banking systems that co-exist in the United States. The federal system is based on a federal bank charter, powers defined under federal law, operation under federal standards, and oversight by a federal supervisor. The state system is characterized by state chartering, bank powers established under state law, and operation under state standards, including oversight by state supervisors.

It has been a bedrock precept of our constitutional law for more than 180 years, since the Supreme Court's decision in *M'Culloch* v. *Maryland* in 1819, that states cannot constitutionally control the powers of entities created under federal law. Courts have consistently applied this principle over the years to national banks, holding a variety of state laws inapplicable to national banks, and finding that the federally authorized powers of national banks are not subject to state supervision and regulation.

Against this background, it is quite surprising to hear supporters of the dual banking system criticizing national banks for utilizing — and the OCC for asserting and defending — the very characteristics of the national bank charter that distinguish national banks from state banks and make the system "dual." It's as if they were saying "We think the dual banking system is great, except for the features that make it dual."

As this paper explains, the OCC's positions on national bank powers and preemption and the OCC's exclusive regulatory authority over national banks are not new. They are deeply rooted in constitutional principles and the history of the national banking system. Preemption of state laws that retard, impede, or obstruct national banks' ability to exercise powers authorized under federal law, and the OCC's extensive, virtually exclusive "visitorial powers" over national banks, **are differences in national and state bank powers and supervisory implementation that are not inconsistent with the dual banking system; they are the defining characteristics of it.**

Early History of the Dual Federal/State Banking System

The banking system in the United States is described as "dual" because it is made up of separate federal and state component systems. This duality has existed in various forms since the earliest years of our nation, and while the federal and state components of the system have evolved in structure over the years, the essential characteristics of the system's duality have not. The federal system is based on a federal bank charter, powers defined under federal law, operation under federal standards, and oversight by a federal supervisor. The state system is characterized by state chartering, bank powers established under state law, and operation under state standards, subject to state supervision. As Professor Kenneth Scott wrote in his landmark analysis of the dual banking system, the "very core of the dual banking system is the simultaneous existence of different regulatory options that are not alike in terms of statutory provisions, regulatory implementation and administrative policy."[1]

Although a system of national banks would not be created until 1863, the need for and desirability of federal banks and their potential role in shaping a national economy were evident from the very beginning of the United States. Initially, the federal component of the dual banking system comprised just one bank — the First Bank of the United States, the brainchild of Alexander Hamilton, the first Secretary of the Treasury. The First Bank operated nationally, through multiple, multi-state offices, from 1791 until 1811. The U.S. government subscribed for 20 percent of its stock, borrowing from the Bank itself in order to buy the stock. The remaining 80 percent of the First Bank was

---

[1] Kenneth E. Scott, *The Dual Banking System: A Model of Competition in Regulation*, 30 Stan. L. Rev. 1, 41 (1977).

owned by private investors, but they were required to use recently issued government bonds to pay 75 percent of their stock subscription price. Thus, in all, 80 percent of the First Bank's original capital was backed by some form of government obligation.

Yet the First Bank actually dealt in government debt only in connection with these transactions at its inception. Its main function was "to provide a large, stable, but flexible national money supply for the financing of ordinary business and economic development . . . . Hamilton insisted that it be operated for the private profit of its stockholders, thus making it in the interest of the stockholders to run it properly."[2] As a check, however, the operations of the First Bank were subject to inspection by the Treasury Department.

The First Bank's charter expired in 1811, but it was revived as the Second Bank of the United States in 1816. The Second Bank was designed to replicate the First Bank in structure and many of its functions. Again, 80 percent of the Bank's capital stock was offered to the investing public, and the remaining 20 percent was purchased by the federal government using various forms of government obligations as consideration. Twenty of the Bank's 25 directors were elected by the stockholders, with five appointed by the President. The Second Bank operated nationally, through a system of branch offices, from 1816 until 1836, at which time President Andrew Jackson blocked renewal of its charter.

---

[2] Forrest McDonald, *Alexander Hamilton, A Biography* 195 (1979).

The Second Bank's most lasting legacy, however, may have been the litigation its activities provoked when the state of Maryland sought to tax its activities. In an effort to stabilize credit and currency, the Bank had begun calling in its loans and tightening its credit policies. This action triggered an intense economic depression, known as the Panic of 1819. States reacted with different measures, including taxation, designed to drive the branches of the Second Bank from their jurisdictions. (States rankled particularly at the fact that, with a charter from the federal government, the Second Bank was able to open branches and operate its business where it pleased, without state permissions.) The Bank resisted the attack from Maryland, and the issue ultimately was resolved by the landmark Supreme Court decision on federal preemption, *M'Culloch* v. *Maryland*,[3] in which the Court declared that "states have no power, by taxation or otherwise, to retard, impede, burden, or in any manner control" the operations of a federally created entity, such as the Second Bank.[4]

During this early period, banks were chartered at the state level, generally through special acts of the state legislatures. Following the demise of the Second Bank, however, the states began to enact "free banking" laws, which permitted organizers to incorporate banks without going through a legislative process, provided they met specified conditions. These free banking laws encouraged the chartering of new state banks and resulted in a dispersed and decentralized state banking system. State banking powers varied state-to-state, and the capacities of state supervision were uneven.

---

[3] *M'Culloch* v. *Maryland*, 17 U.S. (4 Wheat.) 316, 436 (1819).

[4] *Id.*

Creation of the National Banking System

The exigencies of the Civil War were the catalyst for President Abraham Lincoln to establish the national banking system, but the origins of the system trace directly to the First and Second Banks of the United States. Lincoln, it will be recalled, "had been a confirmed Whig and a follower of Henry Clay,"[5] before the Whig Party waned, and he joined the newly created Republican Party. The centerpiece of the Whig party's nationalist economic program in the early to mid-1800s was Clay's "American System," a visionary program of national economic development that included federal construction of interstate turnpikes and canals, federal funding for other internal improvements, protective tariffs to nurture fledgling domestic industries, **and a national bank**. The American System, including its national bank component, in turn, traced its lineage to the economic policies and programs of Alexander Hamilton.[6] Clay fought for, but lost, the battle over re-chartering of the Second Bank of the United States in the 1830s, but he and the Whigs continued to advocate the importance of a national bank in order to stabilize the currency and money supply and provide needed credit to support national economic growth.

Lincoln did not forget Clay's political legacy,[7] and in the midst of his first administration, he sent to Congress legislation to establish the national banking system. But

---

[5] Maurice G. Baxter, *Henry Clay and the American System* 209 (1995).

[6] Of the link between Clay and Hamilton, it has been written that Clay "made Federalism a living vision, replacing the dry logical prose of Hamilton with thrilling pictures of a glorious future. The blaze of nationalism suggested a new and disarming name – the American System – and under Clay's solicitous care, this rebaptized Federalism slowly won its way to the inner councils of the government." Arthur M. Schlesinger, Jr., *The Age of Jackson* 12 (1945).

[7] In 1861, after his election to the presidency and shortly before his first inauguration, Lincoln recalled how he "loved and revered [Clay] as a teacher and leader." 4 *The Collected Works of Abraham Lincoln* 184 (Roy P. Basler, ed., 1953) (letter from Lincoln to James Sulgrove, Jan. 28, 1861). A year and a half later, mired in the midst of the Civil War, Lincoln acknowledged a memento sent to him by one of Clay's sons, and wrote of Clay, "I recognize his voice, speaking as it ever spoke, for the Union, the Constitution, and the freedom of mankind." *Abraham Lincoln: His Speeches and Writings* 651 (Roy P. Basler, ed., 1946) (letter from Lincoln to John Clay, Aug. 9, 1862). Five months later, Lincoln sent to Congress legislation to establish the national banking system.

rather than revive the First Bank and Second Bank model of a single large, big city-based bank with (unpopular) branch locations intruding into multiple states, Lincoln borrowed the separate bank incorporation concept from state free-banking statutes. The new national banking system accordingly was designed to be made up of many separate, federally chartered, privately owned, and **locally** managed banks that would be established throughout the country.

Yet, while this new national system would function via multiple federal charters, its constituent parts shared the same essential federal character as their First and Second Bank predecessors. They operated pursuant to a federal charter, but were privately controlled and managed. Wherever located, they would exercise a uniform set of federal powers, under federal standards of operation, and federally mandated capitalization, with a federal supervisor overseeing all of the foregoing. The new national banks also were required to buy Treasury securities as a portion of their capitalization — providing the federal government with a vital source of funds to finance its Civil War effort — and these securities, in turn, were pledged as backing for a new species of circulating notes issued by the banks with the Comptroller's approval. Backed by government securities, these circulating notes were designed to be the new national currency that would hold a stable value and could be used, reliably, across the nation. Thus, while the Civil War provided the catalyst for establishing a new system of national banks, the national banking system was more than just a financing arm for the government's war effort. It was part of a national program of economic development, expounded by Henry Clay, traceable to Alexander Hamilton, finally implemented by Lincoln.[8]

---

[8] Baxter, *supra*, at 209, 210 ("During the Civil War, a decade after the Kentuckian's death . . . Lincoln and the Republican Party implemented much of the American System.").

What Makes the Dual Banking System Dual?

From the very outset, therefore, national banks were unique federal creations. Beyond their short-term role in Civil War finance, this was a system of financial institutions with a distinct pedigree, designed to far outlast the financial requirements of the War, with attributes of uniformity and stability intended to foster commerce throughout the nation in furtherance of a strong national economy. The uniformity of powers and operating standards established for national banks under the National Bank Act — assured through preemption of any state laws that would attempt to "retard, impede, burden, or in any manner control" their federally authorized activities — coupled with the OCC's exclusive supervisory and regulatory authority, have been defining characteristics of national banks from their inception. Together, these characteristics constitute essential distinctions between the national banking system and the system of state-chartered and state-regulated banks that make up the other half of our dual banking system.

Ironically, many opponents of preemption are also ardent defenders of the "dual banking system." It is perplexing to hear those advocates on the one hand embracing the "dual banking system," while at the same time criticizing national banks for asserting — and the OCC for defending — the very characteristics of the national bank charter that distinguish national and state banks and make the system "dual." These commentators praise the state banking system because of the **variety** of activities that may be allowed in different states. It is said that the **varied** powers and regulatory approaches possible in different states enable state systems to serve as laboratories for innovation and that this potential diversity of standards is a valued attribute of the state component of the dual banking system. But then these same commentators criticize the other half of the dual banking system — national banks — for seeking **national** standards of operation and supervision, consistent with the **national** character of their charter and their supervisor. It's as if they were saying "We think the dual banking system is great, except for the features that make it dual."

Preemption of state laws that would "retard, impede, burden, or in any manner control" national banks' ability to exercise powers authorized under federal law, and the OCC's extensive, virtually exclusive "visitorial powers" over national banks, **are differences in national and state bank powers and supervisory implementation that are not inconsistent with the dual banking system; they are the defining characteristics of it.** Those that resist or try to blur those distinctions effectively undermine the character of the dual banking system.

Benefits of the Distinctions Between the National and State Banking Systems

Each component of the dual banking system makes different, positive contributions to the overall strength of the U.S. banking system, and efforts to dilute the unique characteristics of one component of the system undermine the collective strength that comes from the diverse contributions of the two systems. Commentators and state bank supervisors rightly assert, for example, that a separate system of state banks "allows the states to serve as laboratories for innovation and change, not only in bank powers and structures, but also in the area of consumer protection."[9] State supervisors also make what is, in effect, a "smaller is better" argument in favor of the attributes of state systems, lauding the physical proximity of state bank regulators to the institutions they supervise, suggesting that state banks have greater access to state regulators and that geographic proximity gives state regulators greater familiarity with the banks they oversee.

On the other hand, the national banking system is the venue for testing and evaluating the efficiencies and benefits that flow from uniform national standards. This takes on a new value as the banking and financial marketplace evolves, increasingly oblivious to state boundaries, as a result of enhanced technology and the growth of national markets for loans, deposits and other financial products. In other words, the national banking system is a laboratory, too, but what it demonstrates is the value of applying uniform national standards to activities and products that, today, have national markets.

---

[9] Testimony of Joseph A. Smith, Jr., North Carolina Commissioner of Banks, on behalf of the Conference of State Bank Supervisors, before the House Committee on Financial Services, June 4, 2003, *available at* http://www.csbs.org/government/legislative/testimony/leg_testimony_060403.htm.

The OCC's nationwide jurisdiction over banks ranging from modest-sized community banks to some of the largest banks in the world also contributes to the agency's ability to develop and maintain highly expert credit examination and risk management capabilities that benefit all sizes and types of banks in the national system. And its nationwide reach enables the OCC to take actions to protect national bank customers regardless of the state in which they reside. In this regard, pioneering steps taken by the OCC to combat unfair or deceptive practices, and the OCC's progressive approach to customer privacy issues, have had nationwide consumer benefits.

Nor do state banking systems hold a monopoly on innovation or on proximity to the banks they supervise. The OCC's resources and depth of expertise have supported major advances in the business of banking through the national bank charter, and the OCC has pioneered a supervisory approach premised on distinctions in the **type of proximity** most appropriate for a given type of bank. Supervision of most national banks, which are community banks, is conducted through a network of over 60 field offices located throughout the country, while the largest, most complex national banks are supervised by teams of examiners actually stationed on premises at those banks.

The benefits of having a dual banking system thus flow from allowing each of the two components of the system to function in accordance with its distinctive attributes. State banking does not deliver the benefits of having separate state systems serve as "laboratories" if state bank powers simply copycat national bank powers, or if state consumer protection standards that would otherwise be applicable to state banks are waived whenever such a law is preempted as applied to a national bank. Nor are the benefits of the attributes of the national system realized if national banks are unable to realize the efficiencies and benefits of operating under uniform national standards and the federal supervisory system.

The following sections discuss the historical background and extensive body of case law that has addressed the attributes of the national bank charter and the national banking system — federal powers, virtually exclusive federal supervision, and the resulting limited applicability of state law — and explain how these characteristics are essential and inherent in the "duality" of the dual banking system.

The Powers of National Banks

The long-range goals of Congress for the national banking system — supporting a stable national currency, financing commerce, acting as private depositories, and generally supporting the nation's economic growth and development — required a type of bank that was not just safe and sound, but whose powers were dynamic and capable of evolving, so that national banks could perform their intended roles, well beyond the Civil War. Key to these powers is language set forth at 12 U.S.C. § 24 (Seventh), which provides that national banks are authorized to exercise "all such incidental powers as shall be necessary to carry on the business of banking; by discounting and negotiating promissory notes, drafts, bills of exchange, and other evidences of debt; by receiving deposits; by buying and selling exchange, coin and bullion; by loaning money on personal security; and by obtaining, issuing, and circulating notes."

Congress had modeled this authority on the bank charter authorized by the New York Free Banking Act, a type of charter that the New York courts explicitly had found to possess flexible and adaptive powers. Shortly before enactment of the National Bank Act, the New York Court of Appeals described the dynamic nature of the New York bank charter, stating that "[t]he implied powers [of a bank] exist by virtue of the grant [to do the banking business], and are not enumerated and defined; because no human sagacity can foresee what implied powers may, in the progress of time, the discovery and perfection of better methods of business, and the evervarying attitude of human relations, be required to give effect to the express powers."[10]

---

[10] *Curtis* v. *Leavitt*, 15 N.Y. 9, 157 (1857).

The specifications of certain banking activities that were contained in the New York banking laws, (and subsequently copied into the National Bank Act) were "eminently useful," but "not indispensable," according to the court in that case. Based on this lineage, in construing the National Bank Act the OCC typically looks to the objectives in addition to simply the mechanics of the Act, approaching the statute, as one commentator put it, as "an architect's drawing and not a set of specifications."[11] As a result, the powers of national banks to engage in the business of banking and activities that are "incidental" thereto have been continually updated and consistently interpreted by the OCC — and accepted by the courts — as evolutionary; capable of developing and adjusting as needed to support the evolving financial and economic needs of the nation.

Any doubt concerning this characterization of the powers of national banks was settled with the Supreme Court's decision in *NationsBank* v. *Variable Annuity Life Insurance Co.* in which the Court expressly held that the "business of banking" is not limited to the enumerated powers in section 24(Seventh) and that the Comptroller has discretion to authorize activities beyond those specifically enumerated in the statute.[12] In the same decision, the Court also reiterated a previous admonition that the Comptroller's determinations regarding the scope of permissible national bank activities pursuant to this authority should be accorded great deference, stating emphatically that "[i]t is settled that courts should give great weight to any reasonable construction of a regulatory statute adopted by the agency charged with enforcement of that statute. The Comptroller of the Currency is charged with the enforcement of banking laws to

---

[11] Henry Harfield, *The National Bank Act and Foreign Trade Practices*, 61 Harv. L. Rev. 782 (1948).

[12] *NationsBank of North Carolina* v. *Variable Annuity Life Ins. Co.*, 513 U.S. 251 (1995).

an extent that warrants the invocation of this principle with respect to his deliberative conclusions as to the meaning of these laws."[13]

So, today, national banks operate pursuant to federal authority contained in a federally granted charter. That authority is recognized as flexible and adaptable to serve changing customer and business needs and desires, and the OCC is uniquely authorized to define and refine the content of the business of banking in order to enable national banks to best serve those evolving needs on a safe and sound basis.

---

[13] *Clarke v. Securities Industry Assn.*, 479 U.S. 388, 403-04 (1987) (quoting *Investment Co. Institute v. Camp*, 401 U.S. 617, 626-27 (1971)).

Background of the OCC's Unique Authority to Supervise and Regulate National Banks

At its inception, it was anticipated, by both proponents and opponents of the new national banking system, that national banks would supersede the existing system of state banks because state banks would convert to national charters in order to issue the new national bank note currency.[14] Given this assumed impact on state banks and the resulting diminution of control by the states over banking in general,[15] and probably remembering the state hostility directed at the First and Second Banks, the proponents of the national banking system were understandably very concerned that states would attempt to undermine the new system by imposing

---

[14] Representative Samuel Hooper, who reported the bill to the House, stated in support of the legislation that one of its purposes was "to render the law [Currency Act] so perfect that the State banks may be induced to organize under it, in preference to continuing under their State charters." Cong. Globe, 38th Cong. 1st Sess. 1256 (Mar. 23, 1864). While he did not believe that the legislation was necessarily harmful to the state bank system, he did "look upon the system of State banks as having outlived its usefulness." _Id_. Opponents of the legislation believed that it was intended to "take from the States . . . all authority whatsoever over their own State banks, and to vest that authority . . . in Washington." Cong. Globe, 38th Cong., 1st Sess. 1267 (Mar. 24, 1864) (statement of Rep. Brooks). Rep. Brooks made that statement to support the idea that the legislation was intended to transfer control over banking from the states to the federal government. Given that the legislation's objective was to replace state banks with national banks, its passage would, in Rep. Brooks' opinion, mean that there would be no state banks left over which the states would have authority. Thus, by observing that the legislation was intended to take authority over state banks from the states, Rep. Brooks was not suggesting that the federal government would have authority over state banks; rather, he was explaining the bill in a context that assumed the demise of state banks. Rep. Pruyn opposed the bill stating that the legislation would "be the greatest blow yet inflicted upon the States." Cong. Globe, 38th Cong., 1st Sess. 1271 (Mar. 24, 1864). _See also_ John Wilson Million, _The Debate on the National Bank Act of 1863_, 2 J. Pol. Econ. 251, 267 (1893-94) regarding the Currency Act. ("Nothing can be more obvious from the debates than that the national system was to supersede the system of state banks.")

[5] _See, e.g., Tiffany_ v. _National Bank of Missouri_, 85 U.S. (18 Wall.) 409, 412-413 (1874) ("It cannot be doubted, in view of the purpose of Congress in providing for the organization of national banking associations, that it was intended to give them a firm footing in the different states where they might be located. It was expected they would come into competition with state banks, and it was intended to give them at least equal advantages in such competition .... National banks have been national favorites. They were established for the purpose, in part, of providing a currency for the whole country, and in part to create a market for the loans of the general government. It could not have been intended, therefore, to expose them to the hazard of unfriendly legislation by the states, or to ruinous competition with state banks."). _See also_ Bray Hammond, _Banks and Politics in America from the Revolution to the Civil War_ 725-34 (1957); Paul Studenski & Herman E. Krooss, _Financial History of the United States_ 155 (1st ed. 1952).

restraints on national bank activities. Remarks of Senator Sumner in 1864, the first year of the national banking system, addressing the prospect of state taxation of national banks, illustrate the sentiment of many legislators of the time. He said, "[C]learly, the bank must not be subjected to any local government, State or municipal; it must be kept absolutely and exclusively under that Government from which it derives its functions."[16]

The allocation of any supervisory responsibility for the new national banking system to the states would have been inconsistent with this need to protect national banks from state interference. Congress, accordingly, established a federal supervisory regime and vested responsibility to carry it out in the newly created OCC. Congress granted the OCC the broad authority "to make a thorough examination into all the affairs of [a national bank],"[17] and solidified this federal supervisory authority by vesting the OCC with exclusive "visitorial" powers over national banks. These provisions assured, among other things, that the OCC would have comprehensive authority to examine all the affairs of a national bank and protect national banks from potential state hostility by establishing that the authority to examine national banks is vested *only* in the OCC, unless otherwise provided by federal law.[18]

---

[16] Cong. Globe, 38th Cong., 1st Sess., at 1893 (Apr. 27, 1864). *See also Anderson v. H&R Block*, 287 F.3d 1038, 1045 (11th Cir. 2002) ("congressional debates amply demonstrate Congress's desire to protect national banks from state legislation . . . .").

[17] Act of June 3, 1864, c. 106, § 54, 13 Stat. 116, codified at 12 U.S.C. § 481.

[18] Writing shortly after the Currency Act and National Bank Act were enacted, then-Secretary of the Treasury, and formerly the first Comptroller of the Currency, Hugh McCulloch observed that "Congress has assumed entire control of the currency of the country, and, to a very considerable extent, of its banking interests, prohibiting the interference of State governments." Cong. Globe, 39th Cong., 1st Sess., Misc. Doc. No. 100, at 2 (Apr. 23, 1866).

The importance of national banks' independence and insulation from state interference — and potential retribution — was highlighted by Congress' next move against state banks. When state banks failed to convert in expected numbers, Congress placed a high tax on state banks' circulating notes in an attempt to drive them out of business. This effort failed when state banks adjusted and shifted from issuing circulating notes to taking deposits and offering checking accounts. State banks survived, the new national banking system grew and prospered, and our current dual banking system took shape.

Recognition of the OCC's Supervisory and Regulatory Role by the Supreme Court and Congress

Consistent with this history, courts have consistently recognized the distinct status of the national banking system and the limits placed on state involvement in national bank supervision and regulation by the National Bank Act. For example, in *Guthrie* v. *Harkness*,[19] the Supreme Court stated that "Congress had in mind, in passing this section [section 484], that in other sections of the law it had made full and complete provision for investigation by the Comptroller of the Currency and examiners appointed by him, and authorizing the appointment of a receiver to take possession of the business with a view to winding up the affairs of the bank. It was the intention that this statute should contain a full code of provisions upon the subject, and that no state law or enactment should undertake to exercise the right of visitation over a national corporation. Except in so far as such corporation was liable to control in the courts of justice, this act was to be the full measure of visitorial power."[20]

The Supreme Court also has recognized the clear intent on the part of Congress to limit the authority of states over national banks precisely so that the nationwide system of banking that was created in the Currency Act could develop and flourish. As the Court stated in *Easton* v. *Iowa*,[21] the National Bank Act "has in view the erection of a system extending throughout the country, and independent, so far as powers conferred are concerned, of state legislation which, if permitted to be applicable, might impose limitations and

---

[19] 199 U.S. 148 (1905).

[20] *Id.* at 159.

[21] 188 U.S. 220 (1903).

restrictions as various and as numerous as the states. . . . If [the states] had such power it would have to be exercised and limited by their own discretion, and confusion would necessarily result from control possessed and exercised by two independent authorities."[22]

The Court in *Farmers' & Mechanics' Bank* v. *Dearing*, similarly found that "States can exercise no control over [national banks] nor in anywise affect their operation, except in so far as Congress may see proper to permit. Anything beyond this is 'an abuse, because it is the usurpation of power which a single State cannot give.'"[23]

Consistent with the need for a uniform system of laws and uniform supervision that would foster the nationwide banking system, courts have interpreted the OCC's visitorial powers expansively. The Supreme Court in *Guthrie*, (citing *First Nat'l Bank of Youngstown* v. *Hughes*[24]) noted that the term "visitorial" as used in section 484 derives from English common law, which used the term "visitation" to refer to "the act of a superior or superintending officer, who visits a corporation to examine into its manner of conducting business, and enforce an observance of its laws and regulations. Burrill defines the word to mean 'inspection; superintendence; direction; regulation.'"[25] "Visitors" of corporations "have power to keep them within the legitimate

---

[22] *Id.* at 229, 232; *see also Marquette Nat'l Bank* v. *First of Omaha Serv. Corp.*, 439 U.S. 299, 314-315 (1978) ("Close examination of the National Bank Act of 1864, its legislative history, and its historical context makes clear that, . . . Congress intended to facilitate . . . a 'national banking system.'" (citation omitted)); *Franklin Nat'l Bank of Franklin Square* v. *New York*, 347 U.S. 373, 375 (1954) (The United States has set up a system of national banks as federal instrumentalities to perform various functions such as providing circulating medium and government credit, as well as financing commerce and acting as private depositories."); *Davis* v. *Elmira Sav. Bank*, 161 U.S. 275, 283 (1896) ("National banks are instrumentalities of the Federal government, created for a public purpose, and as such necessarily subject to the paramount authority of the United States.").

[23] *Farmers' & Mechanics' Nat'l Bank* v. *Dearing*, 91 U.S. 29, 34 (1875).

[24] 6 F. 737, 740 (6th Cir. 1881), *appeal dismissed*, 106 U.S. 523 (1883).

[25] *Guthrie*, 199 U.S. at 158. *See also Peoples Bank of Danville* v. *Williams*, 449 F. Supp. 254, 259 (W.D. Va. 1978) (visitorial powers involve the exercise of the right of inspection, superintendence, direction, or regulation over a bank's affairs).

sphere of their operations, and to correct all abuses of authority, and to nullify all irregular proceedings."[26] The *Guthrie* Court also specifically noted that visitorial powers include bringing "judicial proceedings" against a corporation to enforce compliance with applicable law.[27] Thus, section 484 establishes the OCC as the exclusive regulator of the business of national banks, except where otherwise provided by federal law.

Congress affirmed the OCC's exclusive visitorial powers in the mid-1990s with respect to national banks operating on an interstate basis in the Riegle–Neal Interstate Banking and Branching Act of 1994 (Riegle–Neal).[28] Riegle–Neal clarifies that interstate branches of national banks are subject to specified types of laws of a "host" state in which the bank has an interstate branch — including consumer protection laws — to the same extent as a bank based in that state, **except when federal law preempts the application of such state laws to national banks**. The statute also makes crystal clear that even when the state law is not preempted, **authority to enforce the state law is vested in the OCC.**[29]

---

[26] *Guthrie*, 199 U.S. at 158.

[27] Enforcement through judicial proceedings was the most common means of exercising the visitorial power to enforce compliance with applicable law at the time section 484 was enacted into law. Administrative actions were not widely used until well into the 20th century.

[28] Pub. L. No. 103-328, 108 Stat. 2338 (Sept. 29, 1994).

[29] *See* 12 U.S.C. 36(f)(1)(B) (The provisions of any State law to which a branch of a national bank is subject under this paragraph shall be enforced, with respect to such branch, by the Comptroller of the Currency.").

History of Federal Preemption of State Laws Applied to Federally Chartered Banks

Closely linked to the issue of how national banks are supervised is the issue of what laws and standards apply to their operations. Preemption of state and local laws, in the context of national banks, is an often misunderstood and mischaracterized question. Fundamentally, national bank preemption issues raise the same question: To what extent are national banks, as federally created and federally supervised enterprises, able to operate under **federal standards?** Individual skirmishes concerning displacement of particular state laws miss the key point: Preemption is a means by which national banks are enabled to operate under the uniform national standards that Congress intended from the very outset of the national banking system. Resistance to preemption is equivalent to resistance to the uniform standards inherent in the national component of the dual banking system.

The doctrine of preemption traces to the very roots of the national banking system. As described above, constitutional principles of federal preemption were recognized by the Supreme Court in the landmark case of *M'Culloch* v. *Maryland*, where the Court held that under the Supremacy Clause of the U.S. Constitution, states "have no power, by taxation or otherwise, to retard, impede, burden, or in any manner control the operations" of an entity created under federal law.[30] The first Comptroller of the Currency invoked these standards in his first report to Congress in 1863,[31] and since that time, courts have applied comparable principles of federal preemption in connection with many aspects of national banks' operations, repeatedly finding

---

[30] *M'Culloch* v. *Maryland*, 17 U.S. (4 Wheat.) 316, 436 (1819).

[31] 1863 *Office of the Comptroller of the Currency First Annual Report to Congress* 53.

that the exercise by federally chartered national banks of their federally authorized powers is ordinarily not subject to confinement by state law.

Preemption is simply the legal theory that enables national banks to operate nationwide, under the uniform national standards, subject to the oversight of a federal regulator, just as Congress originally intended. As the Supreme Court noted in 1939, in *Deitrick v. Greaney*, "[t]he National Bank Act constitutes 'by itself a complete system for the establishment and government of National Banks.'"[32] In a much earlier case, decided in 1896, the Supreme Court stated that "[n]ational banks are instrumentalities of the Federal government, created for a public purpose, and as such necessarily subject to the paramount authority of the United States. It follows that an attempt by a state to define their duties or control the conduct of their affairs is absolutely void, wherever such attempted exercise of authority expressly conflicts with the laws of the United States, and either frustrates the purpose of the national legislation, or impairs the efficiency of these agencies of the Federal government to discharge the duties for the performance of which they were created."[33]

Independence from state direction and control both reflects the essential federal character of national banks and protects them from conflicting local laws that may undermine the uniform, nationwide character of the national banking system. Indeed, the Supreme Court consistently has held that subjecting national banks' exercise of their federally authorized powers to state regulation or supervision would

---

[32] 309 U.S. 190, 194 (1939).

[33] *Davis v. Elmira Sav. Bank*, 161 U.S. 275, 283 (1896).

be inconsistent with the system that Congress designed.[34] The Court also has recognized that because national banks are federal creations, state law aimed at regulating national banks and their activities applies to national banks only when Congress directs that result,[35] and, as the Court said in 1875, in *Farmers' & Mechanics' National Bank*, "the States can exercise no control over them, nor in anywise affect their operation, except in so far as Congress may see proper to permit."[36]

The Court's decisions also have agreed that Congress was concerned not only with the application of certain states' laws to individual national banks but also with the application of *multiple* states' standards, which would undermine the uniform, national character of the powers of national banks throughout the system. This point was highlighted by the Supreme Court in 1891, in *Talbott* v. *Silver Bow County Commissioners* where the Court stressed that the "entire body of the Statute respecting national banks, emphasize that which the character of the system implies — an intent to create a national banking system co-extensive with the territorial limits of the United States, and with

---

[34] *See, e.g., Marquette Nat'l Bank* v. *First of Omaha Serv. Corp.*, 439 U.S. 299, 314-315 (1978)("Congress intended to facilitate . . . a 'national banking system.'"); *First Nat'l Bank of San Jose* v. *California*, 262 U.S. 366, 369 (1923) (national banks are instrumentalities of the Federal government; "any attempt by a State to define their duties or control the conduct of their affairs is void whenever it conflicts with the laws of the United States or frustrates the purposes of the national legislation or impairs the efficiency of the bank to discharge the duties for which it was created.").

[35] Of course, Congress may specifically require the application of state law to national banks for certain purposes. *See, e.g.*, 12 U.S.C. 92a(a) (the extent of a national bank's fiduciary powers is determined by reference to the law of the state where the national bank is located). Congress may also, more generally, establish standards that govern when state law will apply to national banks' activities. *See, e.g.*, 15 U.S.C. 6701 (codification of section 104 of the Gramm–Leach–Bliley Act, which establishes standards for determining the applicability of state law to different types of activities conducted by national banks, other insured depository institutions, and their affiliates). In such cases, the OCC applies the law or the standards that Congress has required or established.

[36] *Farmers' & Mechanics' Nat'l Bank* v. *Dearing*, 91 U.S. 29, 34 (1875).

uniform operation within those limits."[37] A similar point was made by the Court 100 years ago, in 1903, in *Easton* v. *Iowa*, which stressed that the national banking system was "a system extending throughout the country, and independent, so far as powers conferred are concerned, of state legislation which, if permitted to be applicable, might impose limitations and restrictions as various and as numerous as the states."[38]

This federal character has consistently informed the decisions of the Supreme Court when the Court has considered whether particular state laws apply to national banks. In the *Barnett* case, for example, the Supreme Court had occasion to review the federal constitutional foundations of the national banking system, and reaffirmed that national bank powers are not normally limited by state law.[39] The Court concluded that "where Congress has not expressly conditioned the grant of 'power' upon a grant of state permission, the Court has ordinarily found that no such condition applies."[40]

---

[37] *Talbott* v. *Silver Bow County Commissioners*, 139 U.S. 438, 443 (1891).

[38] *Easton* v. *Iowa*, 188 U.S. 220, 229 (1903).

[39] *Barnett Bank of Marion County, N.A.* v. *Nelson*, 517 U.S. 25, 32 (1996) (the history of the legal concept of national bank powers "is one of interpreting grants of both enumerated and incidental 'powers' to national banks as grants of authority not normally limited by, but rather ordinarily pre-empting, contrary state law'"). *See also Franklin Nat'l Bank*, 347 U.S. at 378 ("We find no indication that Congress intended to make this phase of national banking [deposit-taking] subject to local restrictions, as it has done by express language in several other instances.").

[40] *Barnett*, 517 U.S. at 34.

Drawing the Line Between State Laws That Are Preempted and Those That Are Not

The foregoing analysis of preemption precedents does not mean that national banks are divorced from the standards of state law in all respects. State laws apply to national banks' activities under circumstances that have been described variously by the courts as not altering or conditioning a national bank's ability to exercise a power that federal law grants to it.[41] In *National Bank v. Commonwealth*, for example, the Court observed that national banks are "subject to the laws of the State, and are governed in their daily course of business far more by the laws of the State than of the Nation. All their contracts are governed and construed by state laws. Their acquisition and transfer of property, their right to collect their debts, and their liability to be sued for debts, are all based on state law."[42] Several years later, in *McClellan v. Chipman*, the Court recalled this principle, noting "the rule being the operation of general state laws upon the dealings and contracts of national banks," but the "exception being the cessation of the operation of such laws whenever they expressly conflict with the laws of the United States or frustrate the purpose for which the national banks were created, or impair their efficiency to discharge the duties imposed upon them by the law of the United States."[43] As the Ninth Circuit recently

---

[41] *See id.* at 33-34.

[42] *National Bank v. Commonwealth*, 76 U.S. (9 Wall.) 353, 362 (1869).

[43] *McClellan v. Chipman*, 164 U.S. 347, 357 (1896).

neatly summarized, "states retain some power to regulate national banks in areas such as contracts, debt collection, acquisition and transfer of property, and taxation, zoning, criminal, and tort law."[44]

Admittedly, the line between types of state laws that are preempted and those that are not "is not always well defined, and is often distinguished by such nice shades of difference on each side as to require the closest scrutiny."[45] Yet, if the Supreme Court's decisions can be synthesized into a general rule, it would be that the types of laws that are _not_ preempted are typically those that do not regulate the manner, content or extent of the activities authorized for national banks under federal law, but rather establish the legal infrastructure around the conduct of that business. In other words, non-preempted state laws are convenient, useful, and in many cases, necessary, for national banks to conduct their federally authorized business, but they do not obstruct or condition the bank's ability to exercise powers granted under federal law.[46]

---

[44] *Bank of America v. City & County of San Francisco*, 309 F.3d 551, 559 (9ᵗʰ Cir. 2002). With regard to state criminal laws, it is important to recognize the distinction drawn by the Supreme Court in *Easton* between "crimes defined and punishable at common law or by the general statutes of a state" and "crimes and offenses cognizable under the authority of the United States." 188 U.S. at 238. The Court stated that "[u]ndoubtedly a state has the legitimate power to define and punish crimes by general laws applicable to all persons within its jurisdiction . . . . But it is without lawful power to make such special laws applicable to banks organized and operating under the laws of the United States." _Id_. at 239 (holding that federal law governing the operations of national banks preempted a state criminal law prohibiting insolvent banks from accepting deposits). In determining whether a particular state law falls into a category of state laws that are not preempted, a state may not immunize a law from preemption simply by applying a criminal penalty to it. Also, notably, "[c]onsumer protection is not reflected in the case law as an area in which the states have traditionally been permitted to regulate national banks." *American Bankers Ass'n v. Lockyer*, 239 F. Supp. 2d 1000, 1016 (E.D. Cal. 2002).

[45] *Waite v. Dowley*, 94 U.S. 527, 533 (1876).

[46] *See Barnett*, 517 U.S. at 33-34.

Conclusion

Distinctions between the national banking system and the state banking system are rooted deep in constitutional principles and our country's formative history. These distinctions are essential to the vitality of the dual banking system and should be encouraged and preserved, not blurred or undercut. Indeed, differences that may be controversial today are at the very heart of the "dual" character of the dual banking system and are inextricably linked to the benefits and success we associate with the dual system.

The OCC bears a heavy responsibility as administrator of the national banking system component of the dual system. The national banking system is designed and premised on the OCC carrying out *multiple* responsibilities that trace to the agency's origins: ensuring the safety and soundness of national banks' operations, guiding the evolution of the business of banking that national banks may conduct, overseeing the standards by which national banks operate, and assuring that national banks are playing an appropriate role in the national economy. In this mix, the safety and soundness of national banks is of obvious importance, as is their competitive viability, but so too is the fairness and integrity national banks display in conducting their business. Our job at the OCC, as Carter Golembe put it in one of his famous commentaries, is "to assure that national banks are safe and sound, competitive and profitable, and capable of serving in the best possible manner the banking needs of their customers." In this regard, we have the unique responsibility — and the privilege — of carrying out a mission initiated by Abraham Lincoln and Alexander Hamilton.

Comptroller of the Currency
Administrator of National Banks

Washington, DC 20219

www.occ.treas.gov